bedroom

essentials

ROS BYAM SHAW

bedroom
essentials

RYLAND
PETERS
& SMALL
London New York

Designer Emilie Ekström
Senior editor Henrietta Heald
Picture research Claire Hector and Emily Westlake
Production Deborah Wehner
Art director Gabriella Le Grazie
Publishing director Alison Starling

10 9 8 7 6 5 4 3 2 1

First published in the USA in 2004 by
Ryland Peters & Small, Inc.
519 Broadway
5th Floor
New York, NY 10012
www.rylandpeters.com

Printed and bound in China.

Library of Congress Cataloging-in-Publication Data
Byam Shaw, Ros.
  Bedroom essentials / Ros Byam Shaw.
    p. cm.
  ISBN 1-84172-604-4
  1. Bedrooms. 2. Interior decoration. I. Title.
  NK2117.B4B93 2004
  747.7'7--dc22
                                        2003016886

contents

getting the

elements right

planning the space

Making a plan sounds dull—the sort of thing your mom might nag you to do, or your teacher might tell you off for not doing. Most of us want quick results. However, as with so many tasks in life, groundwork pays off. Unless you live in a house with plenty of generously proportioned rooms, your bedroom will have to fulfill more than one role. In addition to being somewhere to go for intimacy, privacy, rest, and sleep, it will probably have to house clothes, shoes, and bags. It may also be the only reliably quiet place in a busy family home and therefore the room where you choose to work.

Above The sleeping platform is a neat solution to separating a bedroom area in a studio.

Left With meticulous planning and careful choice of furniture, working and sleeping spaces can be elegantly combined.

Opposite, left Storage and bed line two walls of this small bedroom. Books and toys are readily accessible on open shelves, while clothes and more toys are tucked away in cupboards. All in all, it is a recipe for that rare thing—a child's bedroom that is easy to keep neat.

Opposite, right A curtained landing has been ingeniously utilized as impromptu guest accommodation.

- The most important piece of furniture is **the bed**. Decide on its size and style first. This is the **starting point** of your plan.

- **Built-in furniture** is almost always a more **efficient** use of space than freestanding.

- Built-in closets can be designed to make **an alcove for the bed**. This is an effective way to make sure that an **armoire does not dominate** a room.

- Clothes will be the main **storage issue**. Measure roughly how much **hanging space** you need before designing a closet. Be generous.

Left Both space-saving and ideal for games, bunk beds remain a perennial favorite with children.
Below The steeply sloping ceiling of a bedroom in the roof is charming, but the arrangement of furniture needs careful consideration in order to minimize bumps on the head.
Opposite Space is a glorious luxury, here emphasized by the expanse of polished wooden floor and the lack of curtains at the tall casement windows. The design of a large room needs just as much care as a small one, but perhaps not quite as much cunning.

Space is always an issue in a bedroom. Usually, the problem is lack of space: how to fit in enough storage around the bed and still leave enough elbow-room to get dressed without having to stand on it.

In a small room there may be only one obvious place to put the bed—but using every scrap of available wall, floor, and underneath space takes a bit more thought and ingenuity. You don't necessarily need to get out the graph paper and tape measure, although it can help, but you do need to sit and think about what goes where before you buy a giant armoire or even a small bedside table; built-in closets might result in a better use of space, and your bedside table might need to double as a desk.

Think about lighting and where you will need to have it. Think about where you would like the radiator (it is not usually difficult or particularly expensive to move a radiator). And don't forget the space that is taken up by closet doors when they are open, or drawers when they are pulled out.

color schemes

The traditional wisdom when choosing a color scheme for a bedroom is to favor colors considered to be gentle, soothing, and therefore sleep-inducing: pastels, creams, off-whites, and neutrals. But color is deeply subjective. While crisp, white linen certainly has the advantage of looking invitingly clean, there is no reason why the rest of the décor should follow suit. A bedroom is essentially a private space and, as such, can be the arena in which to express entirely personal taste.

Above Chaste white walls are strongly contrasted with the rich strawberry red of bed linen and the strong purple of the bedside shelf. The effect is simple and dramatic.
Left Pastels, traditionally thought the most suitable bedroom shades, are used here to elegant effect.
Opposite The snowy bed linen in this theatrical room looks whiter than white in contrast with the scarlet of the walls, the purple suede of the headboard, and the midnight-black background of the mural above.

It is difficult to prove, but nevertheless generally accepted, that colors can have a direct effect on emotions. However, the rules are far from universal. After all, who can say what the color one person sees as red looks like to anyone else? Of all rooms in the home, your bedroom should be the one where you feel most free to indulge in the red that warms your heart, the blue that makes you smile.

Another, less personal aspect of color is its ability to create certain optical effects. Pale and receding colors from the blue and green side of the color spectrum tend to make spaces expand, while warm, "advancing" colors—ranging from red through orange to yellow—pull walls in around the observer.

For creating a sense of space and increasing light, you cannot beat that most popular and innocuous of non-colors, white. But an all-white scheme can be too dazzling and clinical for a room in which you want to feel safely cocooned.

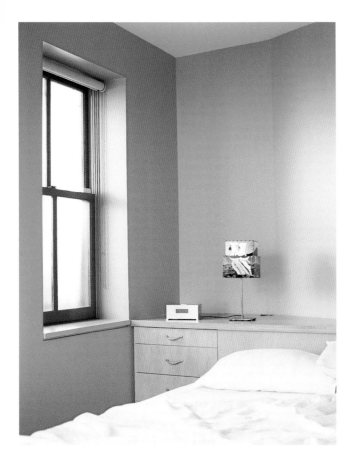

Instead, you can use white walls, or a more forgiving off-white, as the blank canvas on which to superimpose other favorite colors, whether you are making sharp contrasts with bright, strong shades or creating a subtler effect with paler, faded, or neutral tones.

The advantage of a white, or near-white, background is that you can make changes when you tire of a particular color scheme. You might even want to introduce a winter and summer palette—with darker, warmer curtains, bedspread, pillows, and rugs to make you feel cozy on icy mornings replaced by gentle pastels for spring and summer.

In recent years the fashion has been for solid fabrics and wall treatments. This ought

Opposite, left Red is a rich, positive color, especially a red that is closer to purple than orange. Pale pink diaphanous curtains go well with this shade of red, and the soft textures of the cushions and wall hanging make the bed look inviting.
Opposite, above right A striped quilt pulls together the color scheme in this sophisticated bedroom.

Opposite, below right The honey-brown hue of natural wood brings warmth to a room with clean, contemporary lines.
Above A pale terracotta wall paint complements the golden tones of a headboard and integral drawers.
Right Different shades of blue give this room a dreamy quality, ideal for rest and relaxation.

to make dealing with color more straightforward. In fact, if everything from the floor covering to the curtains is a single color, particular care must be given to the balance between these different shades and to the way they interact with one another. The latter is more difficult to predict than you might imagine. Simply holding a piece of fabric against a paint chart never tells the whole story. In this situation, a useful tool is a color board—a pinboard to which you can attach samples of fabric, carpet, and paint to see how well they coexist. The larger the samples and expanses of paint, the more accurately you will be able to predict the finished effect.

Above A disciplined color scheme gives a room a certain formality as well as a deep sense of calm. The very strong contrast in this room between the dark walls, headboard, and pillow borders and the bright white paintwork and snowy bedspread is mitigated by the mid-tone of the natural wood floor.

Above right Neutral tones have a more relaxed feel because there is less play on contrast.

Right and opposite The effects of contrast are softened in this room, which draws from a palette of whites, off-whites, and soft gray. Texture adds both visual and tactile interest to a study in monochrome.

• A **flourish of pattern** in a room dominated by solids can add **coherence** to a color scheme—for example, **a faded chintz** that brings together the pale wood of the floorboards and the lilac of the walls, or **a multi-colored stripe** that links more contrasting shades.

• Paint **a large piece of cardboard** with the shade of paint you are considering and prop it against **all the walls** of the room in turn. It won't look **quite the same** in one position as in another.

• Colors vary depending on **how they are lit**. A bedroom color should look good in artificial and **natural light**.

Below Apart from the bed, storage is the most important element of the furnishings in any bedroom. Built-in closets are an extremely efficient use of space and, as here, can combine sections for hanging and folding as well as that bedroom essential, a full-length mirror. There are many excellent modular lines that can be purchased off the peg and put together to suit personal requirements, and they tend to be less expensive than made-to-measure systems.

Above The style of bed you choose will be the key to the decoration of the room. Here the feel is robust and almost industrial: a metal bedstead, which uses poles and connectors reminiscent of scaffolding, sheltering under a metal spiral staircase, which may once have been a fire escape.
Opposite A completely plain low divan, dressed in white, evokes a mood of meditative simplicity—an effect reinforced by the restrained, almost monastic architecture of the room.

furniture & storage

Whether it is a modern divan or an antique extravaganza, the bed remains the central feature of any bedroom, and is likely to be the single most expensive item of furniture in the room. While a bed's appearance will set the style for the décor, its comfort is equally important. Choosing the right mattress is not simply a question of insuring a good night's sleep; it can also prevent back problems. If you prefer a soft mattress, choose a bed with a sprung divan base. Mattresses suitable for laying on wooden slats tend to be much firmer. Whatever kind of mattress you invest in, remember to turn it a couple of times a year to keep the wear evenly spread.

Antique bedsteads can be irresistibly beautiful but apparently impractical, since they are rarely a standard size—Victorian double beds, for example, are often far too narrow to satisfy modern notions of king-sized comfort. However, a Victorian double bed can make a pleasantly generous 21st-century single and, even if you cannot find a bedspread of exactly the right size, there are companies which will make a mattress to fit an old bed frame for a price that compares favorably with a good-quality standard mattress.

Second only in importance to the bed is storage. Many of us lack a separate dressing-room or a walk-in closet, so somewhere to keep clothes fresh and dust-free must be found in the bedroom itself. Never before have so many people owned so many clothes. Where once a few hooks and a wooden chest would have sufficed, we now require ranks of drawers, tiers of shoe racks, and yards of clothesrod.

Opposite, left Sleeping space in this warehouse conversion can be set up almost anywhere—all it takes is a couple of tatami mats, futons, pillows, and a well-placed chair.

Left and below A stylish headboard gives presence to a simple divan—and makes it more comfortable to sit up in bed. The plain upholstered headboard (left) looks clean and contemporary, while the huge piece of roughly carved wood (below) seems to shelter the bed as well as giving the room character with its organic shape and beautiful grain.

Right and far right, top and middle Carefully laundered and folded bed linen offers an aesthetic pleasure.

Far right, bottom A bedside table should be big enough to hold books and a glass of water.

Freestanding armoires can be purchased in all shapes, sizes, and styles—from cheap-and-cheerful zip-up fabric modules to a cedar-lined behemoth. Similarly, chests and chests-of-drawers can consist of anything from valuable antiques to painted composite board. Antique pieces are not necessarily more expensive than good-quality new furniture, but antique armoires that predate 1900 tend to be too narrow for modern coathangers. And don't buy an old armoire or chest that smells of mothballs—or your clothes will ever after smell like great-grandmother's attic.

A large bedroom can accommodate freestanding armoires and chests, but in small rooms built-in closets will give you a lot more volume per square foot of floor space. Built-in closets can reach right up to the ceiling and into corners and alcoves. You can build in cabinets along a whole wall, or design them to flank the bed with high storage across the top, making a recess into which the headboard fits. Inevitably, this will mean that some cupboards are more easily accessible than others, and you will probably find that a certain amount of juggling is a biannual necessity—packing summer clothes into boxes banished to high shelves in the winter and doing the same with bulky woolens in the summer.

Labeling boxes in which you keep things for infrequent use can save a lot of time and rummaging. A Polaroid photograph attached to the front of stacked boxes of shoes provides a neat form of quick identification.

Once you have somewhere to lay your head and hang your jacket, additional furnishings are more a question of space and choice than necessity. At the top of the list should be a bedside table, providing an invaluable surface for a reading

Opposite, above left A wood-paneled bedroom is enriched by iconic pieces of 20th-century design: an undulating screen by Charles Eames, and a leather upholstered chaise by Edward Wormley.

Opposite, above right An antique wooden chest, probably designed to hold documents, looks entirely at home in a modern bedroom, while its shallow drawers make ideal storage for socks, ties, and other small items of clothing.

Opposite, below Custommade storage, like this sleek wall of closets and drawers, can be designed precisely to suit requirements, giving the right mix of hanging space, shelf space, and drawer space.

Above A decorative feature has been made of the storage in this Shaker-style bedroom. Ranks of drawers have been fitted into a recess where you might expect to see a closet. Dotted with the dark spots of their handles, they create a pleasing geometry, but remembering what is kept in each of them must be a daily challenge.

Left and far left Strikingly modern closets make a bold statement in the bedroom of this otherwise traditionally furnished period house. The deep doors contain extra storage and swing open to reveal hanging space and open drawers.

light, book, alarm clock, and glass of water. Even a little corner shelf can save you having to fumble under the bed to find a tissue or turn off the beeping at 7 A.M. sharp. If there is room for only one other item of furniture, it should probably be a chair—not just for sitting on to tie up your shoes or paint your toenails, but as somewhere to drape a throw or put your clothes overnight.

If you still have empty floor space, you can add more furnishings, either useful pieces, such as a small desk, or primarily decorative ones, such as a pretty screen or indulgent chaise longue. Soft furnishings in a bedroom give it the feel of a boudoir—a haven to which you might retreat in the middle of the day, not only when you are ready for bed.

Above A modern interpretation of the Shaker drawers on page 23, these square drawers are ideal for bulky sweaters and jeans.
Left Box shelving in a child's bedroom can be used for books, toys, and games. Artfully arranged, it looks attractive, too.
Far left A bedside table with a cupboard and drawer is doubly useful. The extra storage means that you can afford to leave its top uncluttered.
Opposite A headboard deep enough to be used as a shelf is a sleek alternative to a bedside table.

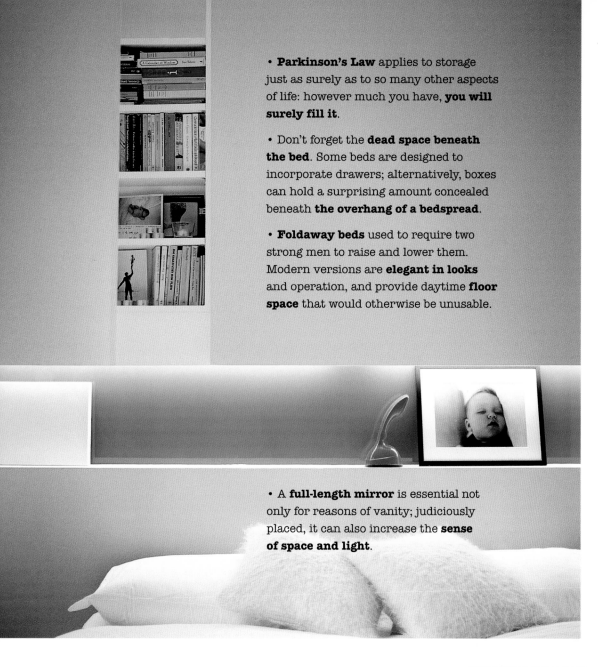

- **Parkinson's Law** applies to storage just as surely as to so many other aspects of life: however much you have, **you will surely fill it**.

- Don't forget the **dead space beneath the bed**. Some beds are designed to incorporate drawers; alternatively, boxes can hold a surprising amount concealed beneath **the overhang of a bedspread**.

- **Foldaway beds** used to require two strong men to raise and lower them. Modern versions are **elegant in looks** and operation, and provide daytime **floor space** that would otherwise be unusable.

- A **full-length mirror** is essential not only for reasons of vanity; judiciously placed, it can also increase the **sense of space and light**.

window treatments
& soft furnishings

The softness and texture of fabrics are essential to a bedroom's comfort. Just as a bed would be very unwelcoming without its sheets and blankets or comforter, an unadorned bedroom window can leave you feeling exposed and unsafe. Not that it is necessary to have acres of billowing fabric. Slatted shutters or blinds might suit your room better. But the style of window treatment you choose will not only be a question of looks; it will also depend on how much light you wish to exclude and how much privacy you need to gain.

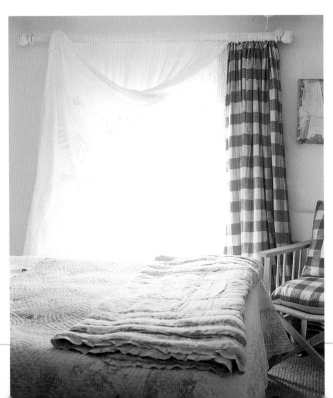

Top These attractive sash windows might have been swamped by curtains. Instead, the owners have chosen blackout shades, which disappear when not in use.
Above Thick wool curtains provide a protective shield for a bed with its back to a window.
Right Bold gingham contrasted with airy white voile makes curtains that are both functional and pretty.
Opposite A wall of window in this sun-flooded room is veiled by sheer cotton. The folds of fabric filter the glare and soften the feel of the space.

Sometimes the only way to achieve the look you want, and make it practical, is to use a combination of fabrics, or fabrics and blinds.

White blackout blinds are an extremely effective means of cutting out light and can be used alone for a minimal look; tucked inside the window embrasure, they barely show at all. However, for daytime privacy, you may prefer to add a layer of sheer curtain. If you would also like to minimize drafts and muffle noise, you can add yet another layer to your window treatment with heavy, lined curtains on top of the sheers—not quite as effective as double glazing, but possibly less expensive.

Once you have decided what you require in terms of function, you can enjoy playing with the aesthetics of your windows. Curtains, whether traditional chintz or crumpled linen, are the most feminine option and tend to make a room feel cozy and cut off from the outside world. Blinds, whether Roman, roll-up or Venetian, have a crisper, cooler look and take up less floor and wall space.

Like curtains, soft furnishings in a bedroom have a cocooning effect. If you have enough floor space for a squashy armchair, a chaise longue, or even a sofa, this is a sure way to make your bedroom an irresistible haven at any time of the day. A chaise longue is particularly appropriate—a piece of furniture specially designed for lazy lounging, ideal for those times when you don't feel ready for bed, but would rather recline than sit up.

- Curtain material does not have to cost a fortune. **Unbleached linen scrim**, used by window cleaners, makes a stylish sheer, and old linen **sheets, lined or unlined**, look fresh and surprisingly modern.

- Make curtains unique with **a contrasting lining** or a wide band of fabric added to the leading edges or **along the bottom**. Aim for an interesting mix.

- Giving a more **architectural look** than curtains or blinds, well-fitting shutters provide good insulation against **light, noise, and weather**.

- You may not have space for a sofa, but you might be able to squeeze in **a small padded ottoman**, giving somewhere to sit and **extra storage** space.

Above Vintage quilts add an extra layer of warmth to a bed, as well as the charm of faded florals.
Right Modern luxury takes the form of a silk-lined throw.
Opposite, above left A generous armchair with its companion stool is an invitation to sit with your feet up.
Opposite, above right Draped over the arm of a chair or the end of a bed, a downy throw represents the perfect accessory for bedroom lounging.
Opposite, below The chaise longue is a piece of furniture specifically designed for resting out of bed and makes an elegant addition to any bedroom.

lighting & display

As any film star will tell you, the difference between good and bad lighting is the difference between flattery and the unvarnished truth. Even the prettiest room is ruined by a harsh overhead light; better to have several ceiling spots, supplemented by table lamps. Bedroom lights should ideally be on a dimmer switch; otherwise, a choice of independent light sources allows you to control the illumination intensity. A strong light is desirable for checking your appearance in the mirror, but otherwise, in a room where you want to feel relaxed, softer lighting is more appropriate. Good directional reading lights are essential if you want to avoid eyestrain.

Left A wall light beside the bed leaves more surface space to put things on; in this instance, there is room for a decorative glass bottle.
Far left The source of light from a bedside illumination should be above the reader's eye level, as in the case of this elegant table lamp.
Below Several different light sources allow maximum flexibility. The paper globe shade softens and diffuses the overhead lighting.
Opposite The simple lines and jaunty angle of a vintage lamp give it a strong presence in a modern bedroom. Its height and position just behind the reader are ideal for comfortable reading.

The right level of artificial light in a room can profoundly affect your comfort, as well as showing the room off at its most attractive.

While some types of light such as recessed spotlights are designed to be unobtrusive, other types can be decorative features in themselves. Obviously, function should take precedence over form—a stunning bedside lamp that gives out a faint green glow is a waste of space. However, given the huge choice of lighting now available, there is no reason why a light that does the job it is designed for should not also look good.

The only exception to the function-before-form rule applies to chandeliers, which may emit a light that is neither pleasing nor useful, but nonetheless make beautiful decorative mobiles hanging from the ceiling.

Closely linked with lighting is display, perhaps the most personal element of any room. As your bedroom is likely to be the space in the home that is least on show, you can please yourself with little decorative flourishes. This might be the place for your collection of handbags or glass candlesticks, for example. To avoid a cluttered look, group collections of things together. A wall of photographs, all in similar frames, looks neater than individual photographs scattered around the room propped on every available surface.

Top left A choice of lettering from old shop signs, arranged according to color and font as opposed to sense, makes a quirky and amusing display on a bedroom wall.
Left A passion for red shoes is on show in this all-white bedroom with its specially designed shelves.

Above Deep suspended shelves in a child's bedroom make books the subject of an attractive display.
Right Where there is no space for a bedside table, as in this room, a wall light is the obvious solution, its switch conveniently positioned just above the pillow.

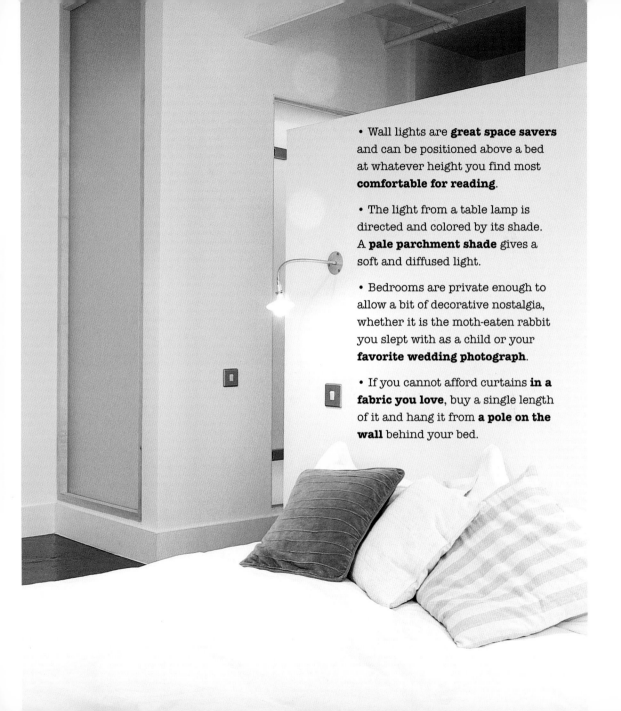

- Wall lights are **great space savers** and can be positioned above a bed at whatever height you find most **comfortable for reading**.

- The light from a table lamp is directed and colored by its shade. A **pale parchment shade** gives a soft and diffused light.

- Bedrooms are private enough to allow a bit of decorative nostalgia, whether it is the moth-eaten rabbit you slept with as a child or your **favorite wedding photograph**.

- If you cannot afford curtains **in a fabric you love**, buy a single length of it and hang it from **a pole on the wall** behind your bed.

putting it

together

contemporary

Minimalism in its purest form is difficult for most people to live with. A less demanding version of the style achieves its effects with clean lines, plain surfaces, and streamlined modern furnishings—for interiors with a calm, contemporary feel. If you want to create this look in a bedroom, it is essential to have ample and efficient storage.

Above Natural materials, such as the wood paneling behind this bed, play a vital part in humanizing the streamlined interior. Simple, sheer curtains filter the light and make a pleasing contrast with the smooth gloss of the wood.
Right The balance between areas of plain color is well judged in this elegant room. The hugely enlarged photograph of a flower adds a striking dash of pattern and some organic curves.
Opposite The straight lines in this neat, stylish room are offset by textured fabrics. In addition to the deeply corded carpet, heavy bedspread, and matching throw pillows, a slightly padded fabric has been used to panel the walls around the bed, making a cleverly integral bedhead.

The contemporary style is ideal for people who enjoy the discipline of perfect tidiness. A plain modern divan, dressed with crisp white bed linen, a simple bedside table and lamp, white walls, plain shades—these are the essential ingredients of a contemporary-style bedroom. But the effect is easily ruined by, say, a clutter of shoes, discarded clothes, or piles of magazines. Everything extraneous needs to be hidden away, ideally behind a wall of sleek cupboard doors.

However, as the pictures on these pages show, to make a room that is both simple and beautiful is a subtle and complicated business. Where you have only a few pieces, it is worth buying the best quality you can afford. The emptier and plainer a room, the more care needs to be taken over balance and contrast, whether between blocks of

Left This small bedroom, sectioned off from a larger room by a sliding door, has been pared down to the essentials. It gets its character from a sculptural armchair, a compelling piece of wall art, and the sloping ceiling with hidden light source.

Above A clean, empty look is far easier to achieve when you have an expanse of floor space to play with. Sticking to a very limited palette of colors also helps. In this room, bright white has been used to contrast with natural wood.

Left and above Painting a wooden floor in a satin-finish floor paint creates a good-looking, durable surface that is plain and relatively inexpensive. The smoky blue-gray used on the floor and walls of this room gives it an almost ethereal quality, as if the bed, with its matching blue-striped linen, were floating in a bubble of color. **Below** The less clutter and color a room contains the more noticeable texture and shape become.

color, or shapes of furniture. For example, pairing a low bed with a tall cupboard can produce a dramatic effect. If the palette is limited to only a few colors, or to shades that are very similar to one another, then different textures are vital in order to provide visual, as well as tactile, variety.

Care must also be taken to make sure that a bedroom in the contemporary style does not feel too hard-edged. Where straight lines predominate, a curve or two will introduce variety of line, just as texture breaks the monotony of color. Use natural materials such as glossy wood, heavy linen, and soft cashmere to offset an impression of austerity. Often the plump mounds of pillows and the soft drape of a bedspread will be enough to counteract the effect of too many right angles.

plain colors, clean lines ...

When less is more, **quality matters**. Buy the best you can afford, particularly when choosing **bed linen and flooring**.

Very plain rooms can give an austere impression. **Use natural materials** to convey a feeling of luxury.

and no clutter

Be disciplined about neatness and **make sure everything has a home**, from shoes and bags to boxes of facial tissues.

Use **balance and contrast**—for example, match a wall of dark wood with a wall of white curtain, a polished concrete floor with **a sheepskin rug**.

Right The exposed wooden framework of this country cottage has been augmented to make simple bunk beds. Clothes hang on pegs, as they did before the advent of the clothes hanger.
Below A floral quilt and a quaint antique lamp provide old-fashioned comfort and convenience.
Opposite New owners have left the interior walls of this 16th-century house almost untouched, with layers of limewash and scraps of wallpaper telling their own story about the history of its decoration. The antique furnishings also have a patina of age and look comfortably at home in their well-worn setting. Only the bed linen and ticking mattress are fresh and new.

country

Country style can be re-created anywhere from a cottage in a field to the interior of a suburban semi. Its essence is a relaxed, quiet nostalgia, and while beams, inglenooks, and uneven walls all add to the charm, they are not essential. Above all, this is a style that allows for the shabby and the quirky alongside simple, traditional furnishings and fabrics.

A country-style bed can be anything from a plain four-poster to a metal bedstead, as long as it is not too grand. An antique will have the patina acquired from years of wear and tear, but there are plenty of good reproduction versions to be found. Add an old-fashioned bedspread over the comforter, or rediscover the pleasures of sheets and blankets. Genuine antique quilts are expensive and often too fragile for daily use, but feather-filled eiderdowns from our grandmothers' era can be found in antique shops and flea markets, and make a pretty addition to any bed (shake them well before you buy just to make sure they are not losing too many feathers).

Since the country look is far from streamlined, it is worth considering freestanding as opposed to built-in storage. Old French armoires are particularly capacious, and antique chests-of-drawers—popular bedroom furnishings for more than 200 years—are plentiful. Good-quality chests-of-drawers are expensive, but you can always find something tatty and do it up yourself. In fact, expensive woods such as mahogany and rosewood don't tend to fit with the country look, which favors cheaper pine or painted furniture, preferably pieces

Left Paneling a room with painted match-boarding gives it instant country charm.
Below Cotton ticking, originally designed for use as mattress and pillow covers, is far too good to hide.
Bottom The contrast of textures between the slightly rough wool blanket and the smooth cotton sheets make this bed look particularly inviting.
Opposite, above left The extra-large squares give this patchwork quilt a modern twist.
Opposite, below left and right Examples of recycling range from painted metal bedsteads from a school dormitory to a new bag made from old French table linen.

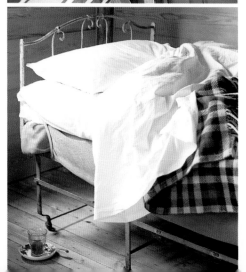

that are a bit chipped and rubbed. Wicker hampers and wooden chests make good storage for spare sheets and blankets or clothes that are out of season.

When looking for fabrics, choose traditional designs in cotton and linen; silks, velvets, and damasks are too opulent for this homespun style. Ginghams, floral chintzes, floral sprigs, and striped tickings all have the right look and feel. If you want to keep the effect really simple, stick to checks or stripes. For a more feminine look, mix in faded florals and monochrome toiles. A rose-scattered curtain trimmed with a border of checked gingham or a striped dust ruffle under a toile bedspread looks pretty as a picture.

Baskets are **light and strong,** and make ideal storage for a country bedroom. Line **a wicker hamper** with cotton and it will also be dust-proof.

Unlined curtains look fresh and simple, and **waft in the breeze** when the window is open. To cut out light use discreet **blackout shades**.

pretty, informal, welcoming . . .

Fresh flowers—whether they are **cowslips in a bottle** or garden roses in a glass vase—add beauty and **the scent of outdoors**.

Wooden floorboards and cotton rugs have **the right rustic feel**, or choose one of the natural mattings **such as coir or seagrass**.

a room for rest

classically elegant

Classical style, derived from Greek and Roman architecture, has been endlessly revived and reworked, adapted to suit 18th-century stately homes and 20th-century town halls. In its purest form it has been the preserve of the rich and powerful. But humbler, more accessible versions of classical style can also be seen in row houses and country cottages.

Left The character of this room is defined by an imposing antique French bed, its dark wood and curvaceous carvings outlined against pure white walls. Barely-there curtains and the lack of any other decoration mean that the bed is the unchallenged focus.

Below This painted chair with its cane seat and back is a copy of an 18th-century design.

Opposite A single piece of furniture can give a room a classical feel. In this bedroom, the piece is an unusual antique cupboard with arched doors flanked by pillars. The restrained color scheme of white and lilac enhances the impression of refinement.

The classically elegant style is sophisticated and serene. In the same way that people who are tall and slim generally find it easier to dress elegantly, so it is a great advantage, if your chosen style is classical, to have rooms with high ceilings. Tall beds, long curtains, tall cabinets—all are practical impossibilities unless you have at least nine vertical feet to play with. So this style is unlikely to be the best choice for a country cottage or an urban basement. However, many small city apartments have been converted from houses that were once rather grand, and these spaces, with their typically tall windows, are well suited to classical elegance.

Height is important not only architecturally; a room furnished with a low divan, a low chest, and nothing that reaches toward the ceiling lacks the necessary formality. A slim four-poster is ideal, perhaps draped with sheer, white cotton or left bare for a more austere look. Well-chosen antiques, whether a single chair or a set of architectural prints, will add to the understated glamour.

Fabrics can be opulent silks and velvets, if you can afford them, but you will achieve a more tranquil effect by keeping colors plain. Stripes in two colors have a strongly classical feel. Simple cotton ticking, lined and made into full-length curtains, can look surprisingly stately. If you want to introduce more pattern, choose a monochrome toile, but don't use too much of it or the room will start to take on a country feel.

Right Painted the color of thick cream, this French headboard is as timelessly chic as a pale linen suit.
Far right Antiques don't have to be opulent to be graceful, as this bentwood chair perfectly illustrates.
Below The tall, tapered posts of the bed and its Shaker-style simplicity set the tone in a room that is both contemporary and classical.
Opposite, above left and right Rooms furnished with antiques often have a soothing sense of permanence – one of the characteristics of the English country house style.
Opposite, below The tall, slim, metal four-poster and the specially made armoire in this bedroom are obviously modern, even though the design of both borrows ideas from antique furniture.

A large **mosquito net**
makes an attractive and
inexpensive bed canopy,
adding **presence and
height** to a simple divan.

A color scheme made
up of whites, off-whites,
and shades of cream is a
recipe for sophistication.

cool, refined . . .

Make a ceiling look higher by painting walls with **wide vertical stripes** in different shades of the same color.

Well-framed photocopies make a surprisingly **convincing substitute for antique prints**. Hang them in a group for maximum impact.

Give closets paneled doors—it will make them look **more architectural**.

traditional and contemporary

small bedrooms

Smallness is usually seen as a disadvantage. But, carefully planned, a small bedroom can become an asset—the ultimate cozy hideaway where you can sleep feeling safe and secure, as snug as a bird in its nest. Bedroom necessities are few: a comfortable bed, a light to read by, a drawer or two, and some hanging space.

Above Older children love sleeping high above floor level, whether in a top bunk or, as here, on a specially made platform bed. Closets have been fitted into the space beneath the bed, leaving maximum floor area for play.

Left This bed has been built on a platform in a small but high-ceilinged space. The wide shelf next to the bed acts as bedside table, dressing table, and book shelf, while the mirrored doors of the storage cupboards double the space visually and reflect light from the window opposite.

Opposite The steeply sloping ceiling of this attic bedroom has been paneled with plywood. The warm color and naturally insulating properties of wood add to the feeling of coziness and enclosure.

The most efficient way to use limited space is with built-in furniture. The majority of small bedrooms have at least one wall that can be fitted floor to ceiling with closets. In an old house, a closet may fit best in the shallow recesses on either side of an original chimney breast. If you place your bed where the fireplace would once have been and continue the closets across the top to make an alcove for the bed, you gain even more storage space. In a room where wall space for storage is at a premium, consider placing the bed with its back to the window.

Beds can be built-in, too, and designed to incorporate storage in that dead space underneath. A deep shelf as a headboard makes a place to put a reading light, books, and a glass of water, freeing up space that would otherwise be taken by bedside tables. Bunk beds are obvious space-savers for children's rooms. Some readymade versions even incorporate desks and sofas underneath. Given adequate ceiling height, a platform bed can be an equally good solution for adults. If the space beneath is used for storage, you have neatly provided two bedroom essentials in a single block.

Right A cozy bed, tucked in at the end of the room, is surrounded by storage. The high ceiling relieves any feeling of claustrophobia.

Below This compact sleeping space is separated from the rest of an apartment by sliding doors which are left open during the day.

Opposite, left When the sofa bed is folded away, this small, bright room converts into a living room and office space. The wall lights and the alcove of box shelving are appropriate to the changing functions of the room.

Opposite, right A spare bedroom has been created on a landing at the top of a steep ladder staircase. The bed folds out of a sleek, modern box and the open lid forms a headboard.

When it comes to décor, there are two routes for a small room: one works to create the illusion of space; the other makes a virtue of necessity by emphasizing its inherently cozy, enclosing qualities. The first demands coherence, plain pale colors, and a strict absence of clutter. A color scheme of neutrals and naturals is soothing and not as demanding, or potentially dazzling first thing in the morning, as brilliant white.

Don't forget the power of mirrors—unrivaled for magnifying light and volume. Sliding mirrored doors can look sleek and modern while giving the illusion that a room is twice its size. Using mirrors to panel small areas of wall and alcoves can make even the most cramped space feel bright and airy.

If you are going for all-out coziness, there is no better way to promote it than with fabric, whether with drapes of wafting voile or the thick folds of heavy linen. It can even be used on the walls, stretched on frames like slightly textured wallpaper.

Sliding doors occupy **less space** than hinged doors. Use them for closets and, if necessary, install **a sliding pocket door** into the room for extra wall space.

Thick full-length curtains use up a great deal of precious floor space. Choose some kind of **window shade** instead.

small is beautiful . . .

small is cozy

Use mirrors to create **an illusion of space**: a wall of mirrored closet doors makes the room look twice as big. Placed opposite a window, they will almost **double the light**.

Your **mother was right**. Make the bed and put things away. Your room **will look bigger**.

resources

ABC Carpet & Home
881–888 Broadway
New York, NY 10003
For a store near you, call
561-279-7777
www.abchome.com
Home furnishings and fabrics.

Avery Boardman
979 3rd Avenue
New York, NY 10021
212-688-6611
www.averyboardman.com
Headboards, plus sofabeds,
daybeds, and trundle beds.

Barneys
6600 Madison Avenue
New York, NY 10021
212-826-8900
www.barneys.com
Home furnishings.

Bed, Bath & Beyond
620 Avenue of the Americas
New York, NY 10011
212-255-3550
www.bedbathandbeyond.com
Everything for bed and bath.

Bloomingdales
1000 Third Avenue
New York, NY 10022
212-705-2000
www.bloomingdales.com
Department store; 24
locations nationwide.

Calico Corners
203 Gale Lane
Kennett Square, PA 19348
800-213-6366
www.calicocorners.com
Designer fabrics. Stores
nationwide and mail order.

California Closets
1000 Fourth Street, Suite 800
San Rafael, CA 94901
415-256-8500
www.calclosets.com
Closet customizations.

Charles P. Rogers
Brass & Iron Beds
55 West 17th Street
New York, NY 10011
800-582-6229
www.charlesprogers.com
Original and restored brass
and iron beds.

The Conran Shop
407 East 59th Street
New York, NY 10022
212-755-9079
www.conran.com
Cutting-edge design.

Crate & Barrel
646 N Michigan Avenue
Chicago, IL 60611
800-996-9960
For a retailer near you, call
800-927-9202
www.crateandbarrel.com
Good-value furniture and
accessories.

Dana Robes
Route 4-A
Lower Shaker Village
Enfield, NH 03748
For a retailer near you,
call 800-722-5036
www.danarobes.com
Shaker-style furniture.

The Fabric Center
485 Electric Avenue
Fitchburg, MA 01420
978-343-4402
A wide variety of decorator
fabrics at discounted prices.
Mail order.

Garnet Hill
231 Main Street
Franconia, NH 03580
www.garnethill.com
800-870-3513
Bed linen in natural fibers,
down duvets, and pillows.

Hancock Fabrics
2605A West Main Street
Tupelo, MS 38801
662-844-7368
www.hancockfabrics.com
America's largest fabric store.

Hold Everything
1309–1311 Second Avenue
New York, NY 10021
212-879-1450
www.williams-sonomainc.com
Everything for storage.

IKEA
Potomac Mills Mall
2700 Potomac Circle
Suite 888
Woodbridge, VA 22192
For a store near you, call
800-254-IKEA
www.ikea.com
Home basics at great prices.

Keepsake Quilting
Route 25B, P.O. Box 1618
Center Harbor
NH 03226-1618
800-865-9458
www.keepsakequilting.com
Good selection of lightweight
cottons. Mail order. Catalog.

Laura Ashley Home Store
171 East Ridgewood Avenue
Ridgewood, NJ 07450
201-670-0686
For a retailer near you,
call 800-367-2000
www.laura-ashleyusa.com
Floral, striped, checked,
solid cottons.

Lexington Home Furnishings
P.O. Box 1008
Lexington, NC 27293-1008
For a retailer near you, call
800-539-4636
www.lexington.com
Home furnishings available
at department stores and
designer showrooms.

Macy's
800-BUY-MACY
www.macys.com
Department store; locations
nationwide.

Martha By Mail
P.O. Box 60060
Tampa, FL 33660-0060
800-950-7130
www.marthabymail.com
Tasteful homewares.

Neiman Marcus
For a store near you, call
888-888-4757
For mail order, call
800-825-8000
www.neimanmarcus.com
Department store;
31 locations nationwide.

Oppenheim's
P.O. Box 29
120 East Main Street
North Manchester
IN 469-62-0052
800-461-6728
Country prints, denim,
chambray, flannel fabrics,
and mill remnants.

Pier One Imports
71 Fifth Avenue
New York, NY 10003
212-206-1911
www.pier1.com
Furniture and accessories.

Pottery Barn
P.O. Box 7044
San Francisco
CA 94120-7044
For a store near you, call
800-922-9934
www.potterybarn.com
Everything from furniture to
decoration details, such as
voile curtains and pillows.

Ralph Lauren Home Collection
1185 Avenue of the Americas
New York, NY 10036
For a retailer near you, call
212-642-8700
Bed linen and homewares.

Restoration Hardware
935 Broadway
New York, NY 10011
212-260-9479
www.restorationhardware.
com
Not just hardware; funky
furnishings and accessories.

Sears, Roebuck
800-MY-SEARS
www.sears.com
Leading retailer of home
products and services
through catalog, retail
outlets, and online store.

ONLINE RESOURCES

www.directlyhome.com
877-898-1086
Wide range of discounted
furniture

www.ebay.com
Internet auctions; every
category of merchandize
represented.

www.furnitureonline.com
800-843-4222
Beds, cabinets, and
bedroom accessories.

www.overstock.com
Bedding, at discounted
prices.

www.totalbedroom.com
All types of beds.

credits

Front jacket Alan Williams/Stanley & Nancy Grossman's apartment in New York designed by Jennifer Post Design.

Page 1 ph Debi Treloar; **2** ph Chris Everard/a house in London designed by Helen Ellery of The Plot London; **3** ph Jan Baldwin/Gabriele Sanders' Long Island home; **4l** ph Jan Baldwin/Peter & Nicole Dawes' apartment, designed by Mullman Seidman Architects; **4c** ph Jan Baldwin/Olivia Douglas & David DiDomenico's apartment in New York, designed by CR Studio Architects, PC; **4r** ph Debi Treloar/new build house in Notting Hill designed by Seth Stein Architects; **5** ph Chris Tubbs/Nickerson–Wakefield House in upstate New York/anderson architects; **6–7** ph Debi Treloar/family home, Bankside, London; **8l** ph Debi Treloar/Elizabeth Alford & Michael Young's loft in New York; **8c** ph Debi Treloar/Sarah Munro and Brian Ayling's home in London; **8–9** ph Chris Everard/Bob & Maureen Macris' apartment on Fifth Avenue in New York designed by Sage Wimer Coombe Architects; **9r** ph Chris Everard/an apartment in London designed by Jo Hagan of Use Architects; **10** ph Jan Baldwin/interior designer Didier Gomez's apartment in Paris; **11a** ph Debi Treloar/Ben Johns & Deb Waterman Johns' house in Georgetown; **11b** ph Chris Tubbs/Vermont Shack/Ross Anderson, anderson architects; **12** ph Debi Treloar/Ian Hogarth's family home; **12–13** ph Alan Williams/Richard Oyarzarbal's apartment in London designed by Urban Research Laboratory; 13r Alan Williams/Selworthy apartment in London designed by Gordana Mandic & Peter Tyler at Buildburo (www.buildburo.co.uk); **14bl** ph Alan Williams/owner of Gloss, Pascale Bredillet's own apartment in London; **14ar** ph Alan Williams/Donata Sartorio's apartment in Milan; **14br** ph Andrew Wood/an apartment in London designed by Littman Goddard Hogarth; **15l** ph Jan Baldwin/a house in New York designed by Brendan Coburn and Joseph Smith from Coburn Architecture; **15r** ph Polly Wreford/Louise Jackson's house in London; **16l** ph Tom Leighton; **16ar** ph James Merrell/Janie Jackson, stylist/designer; **16br** & **17** ph Alan Williams/Katie Bassford King's house in London designed by Touch Interior Design; **18l** ph Chris Everard/Jo Warman—Interior Concepts; **18–19** ph Jan Baldwin/Emma Wilson's house in London; **19** ph Chris Everard/apartment in New York designed by Gabellini Associates; **20l** ph Andrew Wood/Johanne Riss' house in Brussels; **20ar** ph Catherine Gratwicke/Claudia Bryant's house in London-headboard designed by Claudia Bryant; **20–21b** ph Chris Everard/an apartment in New York designed by Steven Learner; **21a** both Tom Leighton; **21c** ph Jan Baldwin; **21b** ph Jan Baldwin/Peter & Nicole Dawes' apartment, designed by Mullman Seidman Architects; **22al** ph Andrew Wood/media executive's house in Los Angeles, architect: Stephen Slan, builder: Ken Duran, furnishings: Russell Simpson, original architect: Carl Maston c.1945; **22ar** ph Jan Baldwin/Emma Wilson's house in London; **22b** ph Debi Treloar; **23a** ph Simon Upton; **23b** both ph Chris Everard/François Muracciole's apartment in

Paris; **24a&bl** ph Chris Everard/Mark Weinstein's apartment in New York designed by Lloyd Schwan; **24br** ph Debi Treloar/Sarah Munro and Brian Ayling's home in London; **25** ph Debi Treloar/family home, Bankside, London; **26** ph Ray Main/Robert Callender & Elizabeth Ogilvie's studio in Fife designed by John C Hope Architects; **27al** ph Jan Baldwin/Olivia Douglas & David DiDomenico's apartment in New York, designed by CR Studio Architects, PC; **27bl** ph Jan Baldwin/designer Chester Jones' house in London; **27r** ph Catherine Gratwicke/designer Caroline Zoob's home in East Sussex; **28al** ph Chris Everard/Central Park West Residence, New York City designed by Bruce Bierman Design, Inc.; **28ar&b** ph Tom Leighton; **29a** ph Catherine Gratwicke; **29b** ph Tom Leighton; **30** ph Chris Everard/apartment of Amy Harte Hossfeld and Martin Hossfeld; **31al** ph Ray Main/Jonathan Reed's apartment in London, light from William Yeoward; **31ar** ph Jan Baldwin/Gabriele Sanders' Long Island home; **31b** ph Chris Everard/Jo Warman—Interior Concepts; **32a&bl** ph Catherine Gratwicke/Laura Stoddart's apartment in London; **32r** ph Debi Treloar; **33** ph Ray Main/a loft in London designed by Nico Rensch, light from SKK; **34–35** ph Chris Everard/Mark Weinstein's apartment in New York designed by Lloyd Schwan; **36** ph Chris Everard/an actor's London home designed by Site Specific; **36–37** ph Andrew Wood/Roger and Suzy Black's apartment in London designed by Johnson Naylor; **37r** ph Chris Everard/Eric De Queker's apartment in Antwerp; **38l** ph Debi Treloar/new build house in Notting Hill designed by Seth Stein Architects; **38r** ph Andrew Wood/Johanne Riss' house in Brussels; **39a** both ph Alan Williams/Alannah Weston's house in London designed by Stickland Coombe Architecture; **39b** ph Jan Baldwin/art dealer Gul Coskun's apartment in London; **40al** ph Jan Baldwin/designer Chester Jones' house in London; **40cl** ph Chris Everard/Jo Warman—Interior Concepts; **40bl** ph Andrew Wood/media executive's house in Los Angeles, architect: Stephen Slan, builder: Ken Duran, furnishings: Russell Simpson, original architect: Carl Maston c.1945; **40r** ph Alan Williams/the architect Voon Wong's own apartment in London; **41al** ph Jan Baldwin/Gabriele Sanders' Long Island home; **41bl** ph Chris Everard/the London apartment of the Sheppard Day Design Partnership; 41ar ph Andrew Wood/Richard and Sue Hare's house in Idaho designed by Mark Pynn A.I.A. of McMillen Pynn Architecture L.L.P.; **42l** ph Chris Tubbs/Daniel Jasiak's home near Biarritz; **42r** ph Christopher Drake/Melanie Thornton's house in Gloucestershire; **43** ph Tom Leighton; **44al** ph Catherine Gratwicke/Rose Hammick's home in London–French antique sheet awning form Kim Sully Antiques, patchwork quilt by Emily Medley, shawl and flip-flops cushion from Grace & Favour, bed from Litvinof & Fawcett; **44bl** ph Tom Leighton; **44r** ph Catherine Gratwicke; **45l** ph Chris Tubbs/Mike and Deborah Geary's beach house in Dorset; **45ar** ph Tom Leighton; **45br** ph Tom Leighton/Mr Hone's 17th-century hutt in Shropshire; **46al** ph Debi Treloar; **46bl** ph Catherine Gratwicke; **46r** ph Simon Upton; **47a** ph Chris Tubbs/Daniel Jasiak's home near Biarritz; **47bl** ph Jan Baldwin/Gabriele Sanders' Long Island home; **47br** ph Chris Tubbs/Vermont Shack/Ross Anderson, anderson architects; **48** ph

Chris Everard/the London apartment of the Sheppard Day Design Partnership; **48–49** ph Alan Williams/Katie Bassford King's house in London designed by Touch Interior Design; **49** ph Jan Baldwin/art dealer Gul Coskun's apartment in London; **50a** both ph Alan Williams/Miv Watts' house in Norfolk; **50b** ph Chris Everard/Lisa & Richard Frisch's apartment in New York designed by Patricia Seidman of Mullman Seidman Architects; **51al** ph Catherine Gratwicke/Martin Barrell & Amanda Sellers' flat, owners of Maisonette, London; **51ar** ph Tom Leighton; **51b** ph Alan Williams/Stanley & Nancy Grossman's apartment in New York designed by Jennifer Post Design; **52ar** ph Jan Baldwin/interior designer Didier Gomez's apartment in Paris; **52c** ph Chris Everard/an apartment in Paris, designed by architect Paul Collier; **52bl** ph Tom Leighton/Roger & Fay Oates' house in Herefordshire; **53l&ar** ph Andrew Wood/Johanne Riss' house in Brussels; **53br** ph Tom Leighton/Roger & Fay Oates' house in Herefordshire; **54** ph Chris Tubbs/ Nickerson–Wakefield House in upstate New York/anderson architects; **55l** ph Chris Everard/an apartment in Milan designed by Tito Canella of Canella & Achilli Architects; **55ar** ph Debi Treloar/Julia & David O'Driscoll's house in London; **56al** ph Chris Everard/an apartment in New York, designed by Mullman Seidman Architects; **56ar** ph Chris Everard/a London apartment designed by architect Gavin Jackson; **56–57** ph Chris Everard/Pemper and Rabiner home in New York, designed by David Khouri of Comma; **57a** ph Chris Tubbs/Vermont Shack/Ross Anderson, anderson architects; **58al** ph Chris Everard/an actor's London home designed by Site Specific; **58bl** ph Debi Treloar/Sophie Eadie's house in London; **58r** ph Chris Everard/Adèle Lakhdari's home in Milan; **59l** ph Chris Everard/a house in London designed by Helen Ellery of The Plot London; **59ar** ph Debi Treloar/Kristiina Ratia and Jeff Gocke's family home in Norwalk, Connecticut; **59br** both ph Chris Everard/architect Jonathan Clark's home in London.

Architects and designers whose work is featured in this book

27.12 Design Ltd
212-727-8169
www.2712design.com
Page 30.

Elizabeth Alford Design
212-385-2185
esa799@banet.net
Page 8l.

anderson architects
212-620-0996
www.andersonarch.com
Pages 5, 11b, 47br, 54, 57a.

Brian Ayling, Artist
+44-(0)20-8802-9853
Pages 8c, 24br.

Joanne Barwick
P.O. Box 982
Boca Grande
Florida 33921
Page 46r.

Bruce Bierman Design, Inc.
212-243-1935
www.biermandesign,com
Page 28al.

Claudia Bryant
+44-(0)20-7602-2852
Page 20ar.

buildburo ltd
+44-(0)20-7352-1092
www.buildburo.co.uk
Page 13r.

Canella & Achilli Architects
+39-(0)24695222
www.canella-achilli.com
Pages 55l, 58r.

Jonathan Clark Architects
+44-(0)7286-5676
jonathan@jonathanclarkarchitects.
co.uk
Page 59br both.

Coburn Architecture
718-875-5052
www.coburnarch.com
Page 15l.

Paul Collier
+33-1-53-72-49-32
paul.collier@architecte.net
Page 52c.

David Khouri
Comma
212-420-7866
www.comma-nyc.com
Pages 56–57.

Coskun Fine Art London
+44-(0)20-7581-9056
www.coskunfineart.com
Pages 39b, 49.

CR Studio Architects, PC
212-989-8187
www.crstudio.com
Pages 4c, 27al.

Dive Architects
+44-(0)20-7407-0955
www.divearchitects.com
Pages 6–7, 25.

Eric De Queker
DQ-Design In Motion
Koninklijkelaan 44
2600 Bercham
Belgium
Page 37r.

Gabellini Associates
212-388-1700
Page 19.

Gloss Ltd
+44-(0)20-8960-4146
pascale@glossltd.u-net.com
Page 14bl.

John C Hope Architects
+44-(0)131-315-2215
Page 26.

Interior Concepts
+44-(0)20-8508-9952
www.jointeriorconcepts.co.uk
Pages 18l, 31b, 40cl.

Gavin Jackson
+44-(0)7050-097561
Page 56ar.

Janie Jackson/Palma Lilac
+44-(0)20-8960-9239
Page 16ar.

Jackson's
+44-(0)20-7792-8336
Page 15r.

Daniel Jasiak
+33-1-45-49-13-56
Pages 42l, 47a.

Johnson Naylor
+44-(0)20-7490-8885
brian.johnson@johnsonnaylor.co.uk
Pages 36–37.

Chester Jones Ltd
+44-(0)20-7498-2717
chester.jones@virgin.net
Pages 27bl, 40al.

Steven Learner Studio
212-741-8583
www.stevenlearnerstudio.com
Pages 20–21b.

Littman Goddard Hogarth
+44-(0)20-7351-7871
www.lgh-architects.co.uk
Pages 12, 14br.

Maisonette
+44-(0)20-8964-8444
maisonetteUK@aol.com
Page 51al.

McMillen Pynn Architecture L.L.P.
208-622-4656
www.sunvalleyachitect.com
Page 41ar.

Emily Medley
emilymedley@mac.com
Page 44al.

Mullman Seidman Architects
212-431-0770
www.mullmanseidman.com
Pages 4l, 21b, 50b, 56al.

François Muracciole
+33-1-43-71-33-03
francois.muracciole@libertysurf.fr
Pages 23b both.

Roger Oates Design
Rugs and Runners Mail Order Catalog:
www.rogeroates.co.uk
Pages 52bl, 53br.

OryGomez
+33-01-44-30-88-23
email: orygomez@free.fr
Pages 10, 52ar.

Helen Ellery
The Plot London
+44-(0)20-7251-8116
www.theplotlondon.com
Pages 2, 59l.

Jennifer Post Design
212-734-7994
jpostdesign@aol.com
Front jacket, page 51b.

Kristiina Ratia Designs
203-852-0027
Page 59ar.

Reed Creative Services Ltd
+44-(0)20-7565-0066
Page 31al.

Nico Rensch
www.architeam.co.uk
Page 33.

Johanne Riss
+32-2-513-0900
Pages 20l, 38r, 53l, 53ar.

Sage Wimer Coombe Architects
212-226-9600
Pages 8–9.

Lloyd Schwan/Design
212-375-0858
lloydschwan@earthlink.net
Pages 24a & bl, 34–35.

Sheppard Day Design Partnership
+44-(0)20-7821-2002
Pages 41bl, 48.

Site Specific Ltd
+44-(0)20-7490-3176
www.sitespecificltd.co.uk
Pages 36, 58al.

Stephen Sian A.I.A.
323-467-4455
Pages 22al, 40bl.

Seth Stein Architects
+44-(0)20-8968-8581
www.sethstein.com
Pages 4r, 38l.

Stickland Coombe Architecture
+44-(0)20-7924-1699
nick@scadesign.freserve.co.uk
Page 39a both.

Touch Interior Design
+44-(0)20-7498-6409
Pages 16br, 17, 48–49.

Urban Research Lab
+44-(0)20-8709-9060
www.urbanresearchlab.com
Pages 12–13.

USE Architects
+44-(0)20-8986-8111
use.arch@virgin.net
Page 9r.

Miv Watts at House Bait
+44-(0)1328-730557
miv.watts@virgin.net
Page 50a both.

Emma Wilson
www.45crossleyst.com
Pages 18–19, 22ar.

Voon Wong Architects
+44-(0)20-7587-0116
voon@btconnect.com
Page 40r.

Caroline Zoob
Commissions +44-(0)1273-479274
Caroline Zoob's work is also available
at: Housepoints, London, UK
+44-(0)20-7978-6445
Page 27r.

index